THE OREGON TRAIL

BY GARY JEFFREY
ILLUSTRATED BY ALESSANDRO POLUZZI

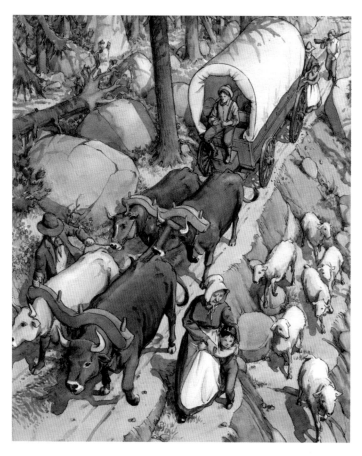

Gareth Stevens
Publishing

Please visit our website, www.garethstevens.com.
For a free color catalog of all our high-quality books,
call toll free 1-800-542-2595 or fax 1-877-542-2596.

Library of Congress Cataloging-in-Publication Data

Jeffrey, Gary.
The Oregon Trail / Gary Jeffrey.
p. cm. — (A graphic history of the American West)
Includes index.
ISBN 978-1-4339-6745-0 (pbk.)
ISBN 978-1-4339-6746-7 (6-pack)
ISBN 978-1-4339-6743-6 (library binding)
1. Oregon National Historic Trail—Comic books, strips, etc.—Juvenile
literature. 2. Immigrants—West (U.S.)—History—19th century—Comic
books, strips, etc.—Juvenile literature. 3. Pioneers—West (U.S.)—History—
19th century—Comic books, strips, etc.—Juvenile literature. 4. Frontier and
pioneer life—West (U.S.)—Comic books, strips, etc.—Juvenile literature. 5.
Overland journeys to the Pacific—Comic books, strips, etc.—Juvenile
literature. 6. West (U.S.)—History—19th century—Comic books, strips,
etc.—Juvenile literature. I. Title.
F597.J44 2012
978'.02—dc23
                                                    2011022835

First Edition

Published in 2012 by
Gareth Stevens Publishing
111 East 14th Street, Suite 349
New York, NY 10003

CPSIA compliance information: Batch #DW12GS: For further information contact Gareth Stevens, New York, New York at 1-800-542-2595.

CONTENTS

THE PROMISED LAND
4

THE OREGON TRAIL
6

THE END OF THE ROAD
22

GLOSSARY
23

INDEX
24

The fabled "Oregon Country" that lay west of the Rockies was first mapped by Lewis and Clark in 1804. In Oregon, they found a rugged land of fast-flowing rivers, dense forests full of game, and many tribes of Native Americans.

Lewis and Clark traveled the Columbia River in Oregon Country on their way to the Pacific.

TRAILBLAZERS

Lewis and Clark's route through the Rockies was far too difficult for wagons. It wasn't until 1824 that a break in the mountains at South Pass was discovered. Still, there was no immediate rush toward emigration. People were afraid to cross the northern plains, which they called the "Great American Desert." Only missionaries and fur trappers dared to make the trip.

The mountain man Jedediah Smith helped discover South Pass.

The first Methodist mission was set up in the 1830s.

OREGON TERRITORY

A wave of emigration in 1843 strengthened America's claim to Oregon, and in 1848, the area was officially handed over by the British. Following a massacre of missionaries, all Oregon's Native Americans had been forced onto reservations. The government was able to throw Oregon Territory open by offering free land to whoever could get there before 1854.

An Umatilla chief from the Blue Mountain area of Oregon

Emigrants used trail guides like this.

WAGONS HO!

The promise of virgin soil, a good climate, and plentiful timber inspired thousands to go. It could take up to three years to save enough money to fund the trip. Supplies for up to six months would have to be carefully stowed in a covered wagon called a prairie schooner.

This painting shows a romantic image of trail life. The reality was often grim and nearly always dangerous.

THE OREGON TRAIL

AMONG THEM IS A FAMILY OF SEVEN CHILDREN, HEADED BY AMELIA STEWART KNIGHT AND HER DOCTOR HUSBAND. THEY ARE FROM MONROE COUNTY, IOWA.

SOMEONE ALWAYS HAS TO DO IT THE HARD WAY.

HE LOOKS LIKE A DROWNED RAT!

AMELIA IS FOUR MONTHS PREGNANT WITH HER EIGHTH CHILD.

THEY CROSS SWOLLEN CREEKS USING A SEALED WAGON BED FOR A FERRY. THE ANIMALS ARE SWUM ACROSS.

THE TRAIL IS FOLLOWING THE NORTH PLATTE RIVER. A LANDMARK CALLED CHIMNEY ROCK SIGNALS THE END OF THE PRAIRIE.

THERE'S NOTHING TO DRINK HERE BUT RIVER WATER.

SOME OF THE EMIGRANTS CARVE THEIR NAMES INTO THE ROCK.

THEY USE A RICKETY BRIDGE TO CROSS THE COLD, CLEAR SWEETWATER RIVER. TOLL - THREE DOLLARS.

THE NEXT DAY, THEY PASS A LANDMARK THE EMIGRANTS CALL "DEVIL'S GATE."

CAMPED BY THE RIVER, AMELIA BUSIES HERSELF SEWING PATCHES WHILE SALT PORK AND BEANS BUBBLE IN THE COOKPOT.

THEY WILL RECROSS THE SWEETWATER MANY MORE TIMES BEFORE THE TRAIL CLIMBS TO...

...SOUTH PASS.

IT WAS COLD ENOUGH LAST NIGHT TO FREEZE OVER THE WATER IN THE BUCKETS.

YUP, IT'S MORE LIKE NOVEMBER THAN JUNE IN THESE MOUNTAINS.

JULY 1. AT THE SUMMIT OF SOUTH PASS, THEY CAN SEE A GREEN VALLEY BELOW.

IT'S CALLED "PACIFIC SPRINGS."

LOOK, THERE'S AN INDIAN VILLAGE!

THEY HAVE CROSSED THE CONTINENTAL DIVIDE. ALL WATERS WILL NOW FLOW WEST.

JULY 22. AT A REST STOP BY THE SNAKE RIVER, AMELIA IS OVERCOME BY THE STENCH OF THE DEAD CATTLE THAT LIE AROUND.

UGH! I DON'T KNOW HOW THEY CAN ALL EAT THEIR BREAKFAST.

LATER THAT DAY, THEIR YOUNGEST CHILD IS NEARLY CRUSHED UNDER THE WAGON WHEELS...

CHATFIELD! YOU JUST HAD A LUCKY ESCAPE!

THEY TRAVEL THROUGH ENDLESS DUSTY PLAINS OF SAGEBRUSH.

SOME OF THEIR CATTLE GET WORN OUT AND DIE.

AUGUST 8. AS LUCY STEWART KNIGHT IS BUSY WATCHING PEOPLE CROSS THE SNAKE RIVER, HER WAGON TRAIN LEAVES WITHOUT HER.

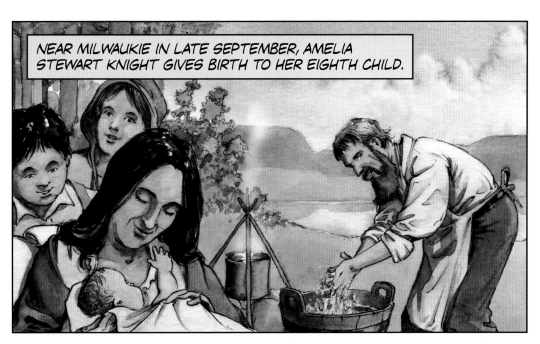

NEAR MILWAUKIE IN LATE SEPTEMBER, AMELIA STEWART KNIGHT GIVES BIRTH TO HER EIGHTH CHILD.

THEY MOVE ON, AND AFTER CROSSING THE COLUMBIA RIVER, MR. KNIGHT TRADES TWO YOKE OF OXEN FOR A HALF SECTION OF LAND WITH A WINDOWLESS LOG CABIN.

OUR NEW HOME.

THE END

The Knights were lucky. Although they came close, they didn't lose anybody on the trip. Others were not so fortunate. Poor camp sanitation meant that cholera and dysentery were rife. During its 20-year heyday, the Oregon Trail claimed more than 20,000 lives—ten graves for every mile.

A map of the trail

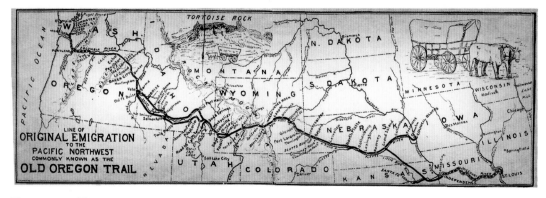

PIONEER DEBT

Without the Oregon Trail and those who braved it, most of the western United States would probably be part of Canada or Mexico today. The eastern emigrants were hugely important in settling Washington, Idaho, California, Nevada, and Utah. Oregon itself gained statehood in 1859.

Tracks of the trail can still be seen in west Wyoming.

The joining of the first Transcontinental Railroad in 1869 meant the Oregon Trail was no longer needed.

GLOSSARY

cholera An infection of the intestine caused by consuming food or water contaminated with bacteria.

dysentery An infection of the intestine caused by bacteria or amoeba that can be fatal if not treated.

emigration To leave one country or region to settle in another.

endure To carry on patiently and put up with something.

heyday The time of greatest popularity, success, or power.

massacre The brutal killing of a large number of humans or animals.

missionaries People sent to do religious or charitable work in a territory.

reservations Areas of land "reserved" for and governed by Native Americans.

rife Widespread, common.

sanitation A system for making an area clean and hygienic to prevent diseases.

scarce In short supply, not enough to meet demand.

summit The highest point of a hill or mountain.

INDEX

B
Blue Mountains, 19

C
California, 16, 22
Canada, 22
Cascade
   Mountains,
   19–20
Chimney Rock, 10
cholera, 22
Columbia River, 4,
   21
Continental Divide,
   the, 15

D
Devil's Gate, 14
dysentery, 22

E
emigrants, 4, 5, 6,
   13, 14, 22

G
graves, 19, 22
Great American
   Desert, the, 4

I
Idaho, 16, 22

Independence
   Rock, 12
Iowa, 7

K
Knight, Amelia
   Stewart, 7, 14, 17,
   21
Knight, Lucy
   Stewart, 18–19

M
Mexico, 22
Milwaukie, 21
missionaries, 4, 5
Missouri River, 6

N
Native Americans,
   4, 5
Nebraska, 8
Nevada, 22
North Platte River,
   10, 12

O
Oregon, 4, 5, 6, 9,
   12, 20, 22

P
Pacific, 4

Pacific Springs, 15
prairie schooner, 5

R
reservations, 5
Rockies, 4

S
sanitation, 22
Sioux, 11
Smith, Jedediah, 4
Snake River, 17–18
Soda Springs, 16
South Pass, 4, 15
Sweetwater River,
   13–14

T
Transcontinental
   Railroad, 22
trappers, 4

U
Umatilla, 5
Utah, 16, 22

W
wagons, 4–6, 10,
   17–20
Washington, 22
Wyoming, 12, 22